Ride the Pink Horse

Poems by Kyle Laws

Stubborn Mule Press
Devil's Elbow, MO
stubbornmulepress.com

Copyright © Kyle Laws, 2019
First Edition 1 3 5 7 9 10 8 6 4 2
ISBN: 978-1-950380-20-6
LCCN: 2019937764

Design, edits and layout: Jason Ryberg
Cover and title page images: Nina Cravens-Fry
Author drawing: Carolyn A. Martinez
All rights reserved. No part of this publication may be reproduced or transmitted in any form or by any means, electronic or mechanical, including photocopying, recording or by info retrieval system, without prior written permission from the author.

Grateful acknowledgment is made to the following publications where these poems first appeared, some in other versions and under different titles:

Abbey: "Nothing Is As Lonely As God on Horseback in the Desert," "Through a Storm"
All the Colors of Life (Kings Estate Press Anthology): "On Hearing the Mahler Symphony No. 5 Performed by Santa Fe Community Orchestra, I Think of O'Keeffe"
Chiron Review: "Esther Doubts What Everyone Else Wants, She Wants Too," "Recipe for Gold," "Red Willows of Taos Begin in San Luis," "Southwest Wink Into Darkness," "Stop-Time," "What Esther Recalls Every Time She Watches a Boxing Match"
Fourth & Sycamore: "Esther Questions Love and Home—or Love and Hate?" "Esther's Last Request"
Leaping Clear: "Going Back to the Childhood Border Between Marsh and Dune, Esther Contemplates Her Future"
Lilipoh: "Leaving Raton Pass"
Lummox Number Two Poetry Anthology 2013 (Lummox Press): "In a Year of Drought"
Lummox Number Seven Poetry Anthology 2018 (Lummox Press): "As the Moon Scours the Stars"
Misfit Magazine: "After *The Prose of the Trans-Siberian,* Blaise Cendrars," "Colorado's Geometry," "Leaving Raton Pass"
Plath Poetry Project: "After a Leg Broken in Three Places," "Track Stretches Into the Distance"
River City Poetry: "Yellow and Pink: Elegy for Jackson C."
Seeing the Experience (ed., David C. Russell, Jr.): "Esther Remembers Banks of a River on Her First Trip West," "Esther Takes the Last Trail Ride of the Season," "Esther Worries As She Cranes Her Neck at the View," "The Way It Feels Around Esther's Waist," "What Esther Is Thinking As Guthrie Rambles His Theories"
Turtle Island Quarterly: "Before the Levee Comes Down"
Visitant Lit: "Cliff Ruins"
Waymark: "Fine Scales *Euxoa auxiliaris,*" "In the Moving Picture I Have of You"

The author would also like to thank the Massachusetts Museum of Contemporary Art (MASS MoCA) for a residency where she worked on these poems and the Boiler House Poets in residency there for their valuable insights.

TABLE OF CONTENTS

The Pink Sash

What Esther Is Thinking As Guthrie
   Rambles His Theories / 1
Esther Worries As She Cranes Her Neck
   at the View / 3
Esther Remembers Banks of a River
   on Her First Trip West / 5
Esther Takes the Last Trail Ride of the Season / 7
Esther Wishes She Had Spent Time in the Missions,
   Even If She Had to Wear a Uniform
   and March in the Band / 9
What Esther Thinks As She Looks
   at Sangre de Cristo Sunsets / 11
Esther Thinks They Would Be Georgia O'Keeffe Clouds / 13
Esther Still Isn't Sure If She Made the Right Call / 15
What Esther Recalls Every Time She Watches
   a Boxing Match / 17
Esther Lived in What Was Called the Castle
   in Garfield Park / 19
Esther's Pink Sash / 21
The Way It Feels Around Esther's Waist / 23
Esther Never Knew What Was Used to Make the Cut,
   but Does Remember the Dewey Decimal System / 25
Esther Remembers the Trick, but Doesn't Remember Why / 27
Going Back to the Childhood Border Between Marsh
   and Dune, Esther Contemplates Her Future / 29

Esther Questions Love and Home—or Love and Hate? / 31
Esther Doubts What Everyone Else Wants,
   She Wants Too / 33
Esther Wonders If Refusing the Bit Leads to Destruction / 35
Esther Tells Guthrie the Only Good Story
   She Knows About Dying / 37
Esther's Last Request / 39

Elegies in Quicksilver and Gold

Recipe for Gold / 42
Nothing Is As Lonely As God on Horseback
   in the Desert / 44
Southwest Wink Into Darkness / 45
Stop-Time / 47
Red Willows of Taos Begin in San Luis / 48
After *The Prose of the Trans-Siberian,* Blaise Cendrars / 49
Colorado's Geometry / 50
Leaving Raton Pass / 51
In the Moving Picture I Have of You / 53
After a Leg Broken in Three Places / 55
As the Moon Scours the Stars / 56
What I Carried With Me When I Boarded / 57
Track Stretches Into the Distance / 59
Cliff Ruins / 60
Through a Storm / 61

In a Year of Drought / 62

Before the Levee Comes Down / 64

On Hearing the Mahler Symphony No. 5 Performed by
    Santa Fe Community Orchestra, I Think of O'Keeffe / 66

One of the Books on the Shelf When Marilyn Monroe Died
    Was Oppenheimer's *The Open Mind* / 68

Fine Scales *Euxoa auxiliaris* / 70

Yellow and Pink: Elegy for Jackson C. / 71

Notes / 73

The Pink Sash

A response to the characters, Guthrie and Esther, in the short story "The Pink Sash" by Eleanor Hallowell Abbott, 1911, about what she is *Obliged to Have* before she's *Willing to Die*.

Dialogue adapted from the story is on the left facing pages.

But once having reached the independent age of thirty, a man's a fool, who doesn't sit down, and roll up his sleeves, and list out, one by one, the things that he wants in the measure of lifetime that's left him — and go ahead and get them!

Why, surely, said the young woman. Something in her matter-of-fact acquiescence made Guthrie smile.

What Esther Is Thinking As Guthrie
Rambles His Theories

The lone cloud in the sky

    is not the only stance against the sun

        but the face of a mountain

            that cannot be climbed.

Ever since you joined our camping party at Laramie, jumping off the train as out of breath as though you'd been running to catch up with us all the way from Boston — indeed, ever since you first wrote me asking full particulars about the whole expedition and begging us to go to the Sierra Nevadas spelled with three 'r's,' I've been utterly consumed with curiosity to know just how old you are.

Thirty years — and one morning, said the young woman.

Esther Worries As She Cranes Her Neck
at the View

How does a woman go into the wilderness

    with all she's brought on her back?

        How does she bear the past?

Of course, at first, she explained, *you think there are just about ten thousand things that you've simply got to have, but when you really narrow them down to just the 'Passions of the Soul,' there really are only eight. At first, it seemed that I could never die happy until I had possessed a very large amethyst brooch.*

Esther Remembers Banks of a River
on Her First Trip West

A handbag spills amethyst and pearls into the dirt

      something to be found by magpies or crows

            or ravens hunched with beak to ground

something you cannot uncover as your wagon

      pushes through dust stirred up in the road

            on the way to the crossing of the Rio Grande.

Things That I, Esther Davidson, Am Really Obliged to Have Before I'm Willing to Die:

No. 1. *A solid summer of horseback riding on a rusty brown pony among scary mountains.*

Esther Takes the Last Trail Ride of the Season

After a night of steel guitar

    and plucks of a stand-up bass

we plan a ride at Bear Basin Ranch

    in the Sangre de Cristo range

aspens bleeding to lemon yellow

    before rifles of the stalk of deer.

No. 2. A year's worth at Oxford in Social Economics.

Esther Wishes She Had Spent Time in the
Missions, Even If She Had to Wear a Uniform
and March in the Band

Reading *Sweet Tooth* by Ian McEwan

      the woman who's found out as a spy studied at Cambridge

where Father's father was from

      but no one mentioned Cambridge when he worked

with the poor in Salvation Army missions

      in the U.S.A.

No. 3. One single, solitary sunset view of the Bay of Naples.

What Esther Thinks As She Looks at Sangre de Cristo Sunsets

From the year of my birth

    my view was of the Delaware Bay

where I sat among ruins of horseshoe crabs

    for an interminable time, watching, waiting

for the dip into the horizon, turned my head

    to answer the waitress's question

about which beer I wanted on tap

    to have it slip away without my notice.

No. 4. A large oil-painting of a cloud — a white, warm, cotton-batting looking, summer Sunday afternoon sort of a cloud.

Esther Thinks They Would Be Georgia O'Keeffe Clouds

A whole bank of them, flat because you are above them

    they below, as it must have looked to those at the controls

of the plane, heads turned and leaning toward the tallest building

    in New York just before it smashed into the side.

No. 5. The ability to buy one life-saving surgical operation for some one who probably wouldn't otherwise have afforded it.

Esther Still Isn't Sure If She Made the Right Call

It doesn't have to be an operation, just a doctor

    who doesn't think a stroke at 87 is a death sentence

even though she's up and talking, a little slow and

    slurred, the day after, and your sister and brother

have had all they can handle and can't care for her

    anymore, and wouldn't want you taking it over

but won't make the decision and ask you to and

    you go against your conscience, knowing you'll

have to live with it, also knowing neither could be

    the one to tell the doctor they agreed to her death.

No. 6. A perfectly good dinner.

What Esther Recalls Every Time She Watches a Boxing Match

Dinner with my mother and sister, Joe Frazier, Denise Menz

    and her mother around a circular oak table in the family

restaurant at the end of Fulling Mill Road. Denise's mother

    is the first to go, then my mother, then Joe Frazier.

What I remember about the dinner is how long it went on

    into the night, how good the Manhattan clam chowder was

and the Jersey corn, and the fried tomatoes just in from the field.

The main course has faded, along with Joe's clarity of speech.

    But I think he said he was pulled over on a back road

between there and Philadelphia by a cop who thought a black

    man shouldn't be driving such a fancy car.

No. 7. A completely happy Christmas.

Esther Lived in What Was Called the Castle in Garfield Park

We must have looked rich and happy at the end of Granby Lane

    with the decorations outside each Christmas—

gingerbread house from a rustic shed, Santa Claus on the ladder

    Mrs. Claus waiting by a pot belly stove for Mr. Claus to

return after deliveries, all of it, and the house, outlined in lights

    while inside was dark as breakers tripped from overloads

dark as schizophrenia of the step-father who put it all up

    and the mother who returned late from working long hours

when we got up on Christmas morning to find them passed out

    from exhaustion and drink.

No. 8. A pink sash. That's all.

Esther's Pink Sash

That sometimes you wear at your waist

    and sometimes you wear at your neck as if a tie.

It should always be worn with black, because

    anything other is girlish, and you are not that

but so much more.

Is — a — pink — sash — exactly a — a — passion? he probed.

Oh, yes, indeed! It's an obsession in my life. It's a groove in my brain. In the middle of the night I wake and find myself sitting bolt upright in bed saying it. The only time I ever took ether I prattled persistently concerning it.

The Way It Feels Around Esther's Waist

Or the way it drapes her neck

      for the sash is silk

and dressed in sequins

      both soft and rough

the way a horse's mane can be

      the way a kiss can be.

And suddenly, my father lifted me high to his shoulders and cried out ecstatically: 'A little child shall lead them!' And with an emphasis on the personal pronoun which I hate to remember even at this remote date, I screamed forth at the top of my lungs: 'I want — a pink sash!'

And didn't you get it?

N-o, she said, I never got it!

Esther Never Knew What Was Used to Make the Cut, but Does Remember the Dewey Decimal System

On the side of the road, what looks to be a field
of sunflowers so determinedly looking east
that I think they are metal sculptures
painted a golden brown.

They stand like soldiers waiting for battle
in another time—not in line like red coats
on the way to Concord, but slightly uneven
as children at the end of recess, about to mature,

before they become Class 5s, not the Class 10 geniuses
resented 50 years later by a man who did not make
the elite class, who still remembers the unfairness
of the system, a paper assigned on the only subject left

after returning from the flu—the Dewey Decimal
System—the one at the bottom of the pile, the one
untaken, and when the teacher gave him a *"D"* saying
it had nothing to do with math, he complained,

It's what you gave me to work with, but that didn't
matter when they were deciding who were geniuses
and who were not, because if you were a genius,
you would have figured something out.

Stupid! she laughed. *What would I do with a pink sash now?* Her eyes traveled down the full length of her scant, rough skirt to the stubbed toes of her battered brown riding boots. *Dust on the highway and chalk in the classroom ....*

Esther Remembers the Trick, but Doesn't Remember Why

She wishes for something other than this town created
out of farmland now a Levittown, where cattle
had grazed and cows were milked,

and someone rose at 5 a.m. to greet the sun,
not the sameness of houses in five models
taunting the one with dreams of battered boots

instead of tight shoes she walks Millbrook Park
in to the back fence to cross up to and over the field
where football is played, their ranch, their spread,

while she waits at the gate for the boy who leaves
her notes through slits in a locker with similar dreams,
and though she doesn't want to take anyone with her,

she doesn't want to be the one to discourage,
doesn't want to squash his dreams, doesn't know
it is a joke until the girls give themselves away

by the questions they ask, give themselves over
to a deception they are no good at, give themselves
up to a normalcy that will follow their lives through.

Psychology is my subject at Varndon College. I have a theory that no child ever does outgrow its ungratified legitimate desires.

Going Back to the Childhood Border Between Marsh and Dune, Esther Contemplates Her Future

She wants more time at the shore
    more time to wander beach and woods
take the day in the curve of land called
    a depression in the sand.

She builds a fort where hawthorns circle
    and gulls cry and rests her back against
white beginning to grey, beginning to bog
    where the sluice drains into the bay.

She wants to solve a mystery so intricate
    she will ultimately go West until it becomes
threads in a Navajo blanket, no loom
    big enough to hold what she spins.

She starts early by herself, sitting as if on a cross-
    country train traveling America
arrives rested if slightly lonely, her mind open
    all the past wrapped up into a larger weave.

It isn't the things that are on your list that astonish me, he remarked. *It's the things that aren't on it that have given me a jolt.*

Such as what?

Why, I'd always supposed that women were inherently domestic, growled Guthrie. *I'd always supposed that Love and Home would figure pretty largely on any woman's 'List of Necessities.'*

Esther Questions Love and Home—or Love and Hate?

The two-fold way a woman feels about home,
both loving the nest created from scraps
found in her neighborhood, a bird with detritus
of years past gathered into something new,
and resenting the obligation of building a nest
for the benefit of others.

I want my things gathered around like snippets
of what a magpie would bring home, bright,
flashy bits of jewelry from flea markets
and craft fairs, all the furniture used,
worn hand rests of chairs, kitchen table
scratched where someone dragged a fork,
bookcases chipped and gouged from moves,
a mattress on the floor but still atop a box spring
because long ago the frame broke and it was so much
easier to put on shoes from that height than before.

And art on all the walls. And leaning against the walls.
And sitting on top of suitcases from every era,
half packed and ready to go. One holds thigh-high nylons
with a gel that grips the legs from when your mother
sent you a black wool skirt and burgundy ankle boots
you were going to wear on New Year's Eve in Paris
the year of the World Trade Center attack and didn't.

Well — eternity sounds so l-long, she stammered, *and I have a perfect horror of going to Heaven on an empty stomach.*

Esther Doubts What Everyone Else Wants, She Wants Too

Being empty, unfilled, unfulfilled is the terror—
long stretches of boredom with no paper and pen,
no typewriter and ribbon, no computer and printer,

in paradise with no tension, nothing to provoke a response,
and so I think about nothing, not even the perfection of trees,
the canopy they form, and no word comes for the kind

of tree they are, because they are all foreign to me,
as paradise is foreign to me, as the desire for paradise
is foreign to me, why I fear Heaven, a place idle and easy,

without effort and strain, no words for what's come before
when all my senses from the time I was born went into how
to make disaster, or its friendlier cousin unease, into art.

You women do not seem to marry any too easily, smiled Guthrie, gazing nervously from his open watch to the furthest corner of the corral, where the preacher's raw-boned pony, nose in air, was stubbornly refusing to take his bit.

Esther Wonders If Refusing the Bit Leads to Destruction

Saga was restless as soon as I got on him,
twisting and turning as much as he could until
I realized too late he wanted a drink from the trough
just as we were ready to leave on the trail into a meadow
centered by aspen, rimmed by pine.

We headed toward Dead Man's Mine, but since
two died there, it should be Dead Men's Mine
but that didn't have the same ring in the 1970s
when they mined Thorium, able to replace
Uranium as fuel for nuclear reactors.

Today, after looking at a hundred photos of atomic
tests in the Atolls, it's the one with men sitting
with goggles in Adirondack chairs that startles
me not that far from mountains that gave the chairs
their name as scientists look off to *Dog, 81 Kilotons,
1951* and I wonder how many died with a variety
of cancers same as the prospectors who wandered
the Nevada desert after *How, 14 Kilotons, 1952.*

How long have you been conscious? he queried in surprise.

The faintest flicker of mischief crossed her haggard face.

Three — days, she acknowledged.

Then why —? began Guthrie.

Esther Tells Guthrie the Only Good Story She Knows About Dying

Where I grew up there was a story told of the woman
who went to die by the sea. She set up a bed by jalousie
windows that she opened wide during the day and cranked
them a quarter closed at night, always a breeze blowing
across her chest.

She was there for each call of gulls in the morning
and each sunset as it spread red across the bay,
how she wanted to die, but it became how she lived.
And it's not that she thought she had a chance, but it was
what she knew to do. She runs the local glass company now.

How did he tell me? mused Guthrie wretchedly. *Why I saw them all powwowing together in the corral, and Andrews looked up and said: 'Say, Guthrie, that little Psychology friend of yours has got typhoid fever. What in thunder are we going to do?'*

Oh, Glory! she complained. *Are they making my coffin already?*

We're going to give you all the air you can breathe.

Esther's Last Request

I'm going to the tallest town in Colorado, drink beer
in a saloon, meet Baby Doe Tabor with a pink sash
across my chest, go down into the Matchless Mine,
bring up a nugget of turquoise in the blue-green
that is a Western sky where it meets a field of grass.

The one thing I ask of you is to put out a brass bed—
or iron painted gold will do— in an open field,
tailings of shafts bored for silver scattered at my feet
and head, quilts piled high on the bed for the chill
of summer nights at 10,000 feet.

And if I'm lucky, I will pass at dawn as crows
leave their roosts in pines and call across the valley
one to the other, making my way to a place I have
yet to imagine, deep breaths of mountain air
tinged with dew as I draw my last.

Elegies in Quicksilver and Gold

Recipe for Gold

Those who are less susceptible to the pleasures of eating, the splendours of apparel or the distractions of society than to meditation and prayer are so rare today that they can be counted. They are despised as madmen, they are banished from communal life, they are known as poets.

—*Lettres d'un Voyageur*, "Letter Nine,"
George Sand, trans. Sacha Rabinovich
and Patricia Thomson

Poet, used freely by Sand
to describe a life as opposed to deed,
a natural instinct to philosophy
as opposed to setting down stanzas
in a form that will survive the editor's hand.

A poet can be the writer
outside the academy,
Matisse capturing the feel
of rooms in which he lives,
Picasso deconstructing the figure
to pull it back together in Cubism,
French Surrealists making over the image
into objects that become desire.

It is taking everything with you,
every nuance of light and shadow,
the observer and the observed,

the clock and the time it records,
the shadow on the wall as sun slips to the horizon,
the torchère behind the Rockies
reflected off clouds after a rain,

the yellows and reds through the prism of Newton,
his alchemist recipe for the color gold:
eggs pricked for yolk drained into a bowl,
to be mixed with quicksilver,
to be poured back into shell,
to be placed under hen for 21 days,
the furnace, the fire to write
as if it's the only thing
that will keep you warm.

Nothing Is As Lonely As God on Horseback in the Desert

All I hear are complaints of saddle sores,
the heat, distance without points
of reference, and the mirages—
those seeming spots of oil on the trail.

I would give anything if those spots
were runoff from cold draft beers
pulled from a silver keg under a bar—
wiped as many times as stars in a desert sky
and still it shines with oil
of the neighbors' hands—
the ones who come to talk after the shift.

That's what I miss—
the men with bravado of a well-worked day,
the women who instead of resenting
the time spent with me
know it clears a way to conscience,
not quite a prayer but a glass raised
to what's just beyond reach
that opens a path,
a way home
to the front door.

Southwest Wink Into Darkness

But there wasn't a sound. Only wind in the trees,
which blew the wires and made the lights go off
and on again as if the house had winked into
the darkness.

—The Great Gatsby, F. Scott Fitzgerald

No trees, only wind in late September,
which blew wires from a pole lower
than it should be, not old growth, but
whatever new there was in New Mexico,
down from Farmington, up from Gallup,
not far from Chaco Canyon as the crow
flies, but by road .... I stop listening
to directions after three minutes.

On painted pew, I look down at Navajo
used by code talkers in World War II,
linguistics not my strength. I have
enough trouble with French and Creole,
my Spanish only slightly better after
three high school years when I told
myself I was coming west. Lights flick
off and on in a pattern not Navajo,
but like the shafts of light in a forest
of stunted trees painted by Emily Carr.

When we discussed the exhibit of three
at breakfast after the Santa Fe Opera,
two women at the table thought Emily
held up better than Kahlo or O'Keeffe.
I remember having similar thoughts
as Todd and Barbara waited while
I stood in front of every painting.
Todd, ever a Dillinger chronicler,
asked if I still wrote of Kahlo, and what
I said was something along the lines
of, *Not now that everyone else does,
I don't write well in a crowd.*

Gatsby's house winked, not strobed
into darkness like a lighthouse on a point.
Lights blink in the stone chapel
over words with too many vowels.
It's the grouping, the crowd, that shorts,
wires twisted around each other whiplashed,
that makes O'Keeffe's simplicity look
shallow, but she was going for what she
looked like standing alone, up on a ridge,
staff and dog at her side.

Stop-Time

Now ... in the stop-time of a photograph, their flaws etched ....
  —*The Mercury Visions of Louis Daguerre*, Dominic Smith

What a viewer doesn't realize when looking
in pond, glass, or mirror is—when a photograph
is shot, the image frozen, it captures the ache
in shoulder that causes it to droop, the smile
held too long, or the morning's argument over tea,
no chance for repositioning, a response so old
we no longer know we do it. What is captured
is before, and when we look at that instant of time,
we do not recognize ourselves because it is not
who we see.

You can hear Georgia and Stieglitz arguing—
Photography is able to flatter or embarrass
the human's ego by registering the fleeting
expression of a moment. But psychological
records registered in this way have nothing
to do with aesthetic significance as it seems
to be understood today,

she favoring the lasting emotion of elongated
curve and line with pigment, and he the honesty
of the moment, as they lie sprawled, conversing,
in the slow-time after love.

Red Willows of Taos Begin in San Luis

Outside San Luis on Colorado 159
before it becomes New Mexico 3

the first red willows begin to appear
where you feed apples from the orchard

planted after your mother died to the horses
that graze below the mesa named for them

horses wild from the time they escaped
the remuda of conquistadors on their way

for gold who veered east to Llano Estacado
translated as staked but were palisaded

plains up from Palo Duro Canyon
where Georgia O'Keeffe would first paint

the West in the panhandle of Texas
while teaching art, seeing what were mirages

in the cascade of alkali, armor clad men
who should have gone north to Blanca Peak

sacred to Navajos, should have dug down
in the dust as it rises in dervishes

not look for roads paved among red willow
and chamisa.

After *The Prose of the Trans-Siberian,* Blaise Cendrars

I forget where I am. I have to remember which direction,
the woman in purple says as she descends the circular stairs,
traveling south or west as you pull from the station in Raton.
The New Mexico landscape flattens into the desert off the pass,
into barbed wire that keep Black Angus and mustangs from
the tracks, the piñons that fruit every five years wide like arms
of a bear protecting her cubs, soil held to ground by short
grasses never plowed—the Dust Bowl never made it this far.

We go south so we can go west, so we can stop at an early
Harvey House in Las Vegas, NM, so we can walk the blocks
from Railroad Avenue to Charlie's Spic and Span Bakery
and Café, this not the Trans-Siberian, but crossing a country
as wide and deep, the locomotive growling at wild turkeys
climbing a butte across from a stone barn, a rusting Chevrolet
coupe beside, and bricks of adobe of a long gone ranch house
totems in the wind a red-tailed hawk glides over.

Colorado's Geometry

Where the roads are perfectly straight
and fields circular if irrigated by pivot,
but dry streambeds meander across plains
and lakes have the irregular hem of a skirt
made in a home economics class required of girls
that three years later becomes box pleated
in brown wool with tweed matched at seams.
Out of nowhere a canyon appears

that you can descend if the tread on your boots
is good enough, river that carved it called Purgatory.
Backed into the cliff is the outline of a house,
adobe gone back to earth, only the foundation left
and stubby poles that carry electricity from the top.
I cannot imagine what drives someone to these depths.

Leaving Raton Pass

We roll on rails into dusty green sagebrush and the yellow
of chamisa, into ground run by antelope and mule tail deer
and the curve of dried creek beds.

No one had any hope of growing wheat here, or alfalfa,
in the flat stretches of baked grasses, a wide swath
between the green-black of pine dotted hills.

The occasional gold of cottonwoods still with leaves waves
along a running creek, highway a ribbon beside in the grey
turned soil of a volcano where tracks were laid.

This is the path of the Santa Fe Trail, the Southwest Chief,
the interstate highway north/south, but before that the route
that led to the Camino Real to Mexico.

The railway system was a new geometry beside dried stalks
of purple aster and black heads of sunflowers after the seeds
were picked by meadowlarks and field mice made nests
in abandoned rail cars used to store hay.

Eight black headed ducks paddle across what's left of the last
rain in a depression in the field. And a flock of starlings
descends into a one crossing town, goats behind houses
gnawing the ground close.

When you travel by train you realize how open America is,
porous, how the water disappears as have people from the land,
more tractor trailers on the long haul,

paths congregated like cattle, like Sunday under a steeple,
like stock tanks under windmills, dust swirls, devil of the plains,
kicking up along roads on All Saints Day for the folks passed on.

In the Moving Picture I Have of You

Color eschewed,
white sock with toes snipped
allow me to point while
black hugs a leg thinner each day,
pink band at top I wanted to use

for the curve of hips
but the uneven drop might offend
so I pull the long Sonoran Poetry Saloon
shirt over eyes clouded like a moon
on the way back from Gallup,

Southwest Chief paralleling Interstate 40
as I wave out the window at guns
and drums and guitars in the back seat,
heart in the car with you
not left at El Rancho Hotel

where I take a *drop in any mailbox*
key as souvenir to lay next to
the brass of St. James Hotel
in a Cimarron, New Mexico room,
holes in the ceiling from the Kid,

and I want to talk over a steak
but instead it's what the Earp
brothers ate passing through
on the way to Arizona,
black-and-white cowboys

running in projectors at movies
that end with Sam Peckinpah's
The Wild Bunch watched from
the back row of a balcony
before I met you.

After a Leg Broken in Three Places

I want to step off into a path of tall grass
flattened just enough by footfalls before me
so I can follow the way to the creek.

I want the sun on the top of my head
to turn freshly washed hair into streaks of red
so that it holds the rim of sunset in its strands.

I want to disappear into the hillock sliced by tracks
so that those who peer down think me swallowed
in the old sea's limestone.

I want to ride a wild horse that wanders the trails
so that I can sit astride in evenings at cliff edge
as a sentinel to stars.

As the Moon Scours the Stars

If the scar were blue instead of red,
it would be a night scar,
a scar of stars in the sky
blackened for more light,
a silver cliff of Colorado scar.

I painted the ceilings of Betty's Costumes
after the costumes were gone,
after it had been gutted and left for dead,
after the sound installation,
after water trickled and geese called and trains rumbled.

It was a dark discount blue of mistakes
put on a shelf
to see if anyone would take them,
created in acoustics without meaning to,
depressions where voices were stored.

And when the doors are closed,
even the two that open inward for carriages,
and you lie back and look at the stars,
there is a rhythm that echoes your breath,
one beat behind asking permission to leave the sky.

What I Carried With Me When I Boarded

Train late out of Albuquerque,
we wait at the station in Las Vegas,
not Nevada, but the town where *Longmire*
was filmed in New Mexico, sheriff's office
in an upper floor across from the Plaza Hotel.

And I forget this is supposed to be Wyoming
when I watch, holed up in my living room
with plate and screws holding an ankle together,
knee broken too, chasing no bad guys
across a cactus-studded landscape.

Each time one of the cast parks on the square
or pulls the shade to look out the window,
I see the eight of us standing in the pavilion
for a photo when we came down
for an overnight stay.

I remember the enchiladas at Charlie's Spic and Span
Bakery and Café before we passed the time
at the station, one departure update
after another, shopped at the antique store
across Railroad Avenue.

When we arrived back in Colorado, I stepped down
onto a modern metal stool at the stop,
light gone from the sky by the delay,
bringing back shadows of what was just outside
the photo, just outside the possible.

Track Stretches Into the Distance

At the junction on the Santa Fe Trail—south
to Raton Pass, west to Pueblo—the train is boarded

before the last call for dinner at white clothed tables
where you can order a flat iron steak as the engine

pulls to Kansas City across plains in a night lit only
by the rush of rigs hauling cattle from the Tuesday

auction at Winter Livestock to slaughterhouses
in Garden and Dodge City, how the identity of towns

can stay the same over centuries, but the kill closer
to the trail, how the low of steers heard out my window

in La Junta nights after I hiked the canyons along the river
spoke by its name to those lost in purgatory.

Cliff Ruins

The canyon of the Rio Grande
on the way from Taos to Ojo
Caliente is burnished gold,
early autumn river a thread
with no needle.

We visit Dennis Hopper earth ships
—tires buried in berms—plan
where the gray water will flow,
almost miss D.H. Lawrence's
banned paintings at La Fonda.

To share four springs under a cliff
of ruins, shards of black and white
pots zigzag like roads that brought
me here in an April rain in 1979,
circling as crow a carrion kill.

I call and call as we pummel
through the desert inhabited by
wild horses and a viridian sage
instead of the purple of Zane Grey.
No one answers.

Able to float in the iron spring
without even an arch of back,
we agreed the entrance to Hades
should serve more than white
wine margaritas and beer.

Through a Storm

Past the stacks of Power Stations 5 and 6,
past the evenly matched tops of the building below
that sit as if suspended in the air
in the shape of boxcars ready to head west
through the canyons flooded by a dam,
past the bridge over the Arkansas River—
is the sky streaked with rain
from the Spanish Peaks to the south to Pikes Peak to the north.

Because it was in the West that I first noticed
you can see rain in the distance,
how it filters the sky like a sieve,
and how if your timing is right you can drive into it.

And it was in the Colorado mountains
surrounding Victor with piles of tailings of gold
that I first knew how you could walk up through clouds,
how it could be grey below and blue once you crested a hill.

It's like being in the middle of your own creation,
having a conversation with your mother and father,
negotiating your arrival,
what they will make of you,
who you will become, your nature,
whether or not you will sit at a window
looking onto a sunset you cannot see
but only imagine through a storm.

In a Year of Drought

In a rocking chair hewn from ponderosa pine,
on the back porch of a Victorian, black walnut trees
planted by a lover along the fence line, I watch
a birdbath half-way across the narrow 37-foot lot.

Wildfires cloud mountains surrounding this steel town,
mill owned by Rockefeller during the massacre at Ludlow
of striking miners that dug the coal to feed the furnaces.

Blackbirds' sheen in the hazy sun reflects like shine
off slag still dumped down hills around the mill in 1976,
slag ground up to fill places hard to water in a town
called *town*—Pueblo, where the boom and bust cycles
of weather matched the fortunes of steel workers.

Some years there was nothing but double shifts
followed by beer in taverns as numerous
as the denominations of churches
from those who came to sweat beside furnaces.

Bessemer was a neighborhood of claw foot tubs
set upright in front yards, painted virgin blue,
      and inside Madonnas stood,
the Guadalupe version brought up from a hillside
in Mexico where roses bloomed white in winter.

The workers worshipped her and brought home
union wages that Rockefeller with his Colorado Militia
never ultimately put down.

Saturday nights we'd drive to watch as slag was dumped
and glowed into the night, a drive-in movie without fee
like the stream of robins, blackbirds, finches and sparrows,
and finally one grey-taupe-sand mourning dove
in a year made holy by a terra cotta bath.

Before the Levee Comes Down

Murals stretch up in the afternoon sun
and what's reflected back into the river
are primary colors painted on the levee
by those who dangled by ropes from the top:
reds, yellows, and blues.

And as the river flows east the blend of primary
becomes secondary: red and yellow become orange,
yellow and blue become green. This is the function
of levee—creation of color as river moves over stones.

Where the river eddies, in the swirl where kayaks
hope not to tangle, are remnants of last night's party:
barbecued pork rinds mingled with burnt twigs.

Underfoot is a crush of rock that is trail. My boots,
thick-soled, can scale the opposite bank. I can pull
myself up by saplings that know there is water,
that have roots enough to get me to a place

where I can see the murals, not in reflection,
but as if atop the horse Lady Godiva strides
that's next to the rendition of Joan of Arc.

Even with the smell of algae, I want to drink
of the river, submerge myself hidden in a cluster
of trees, know that as I arch my back to rinse hair
of debris, green will trickle into my mouth.

I stumble down the wooded bank, take off boots
and orange-ringed socks, watch paintings for what
could be the last time while feet whiten cold and
stiff in the river from a slip of rock that extends
into the Arkansas on its way to Kansas.

On Hearing the Mahler Symphony No. 5 Performed by Santa Fe Community Orchestra, I Think of O'Keeffe

i.
Funereal, a lone horn,
a life underscored with a black door
in an adobe wall left standing
on a property for which she bargained
ten years with the Catholic Church.

A view onto the flat topped Pedernal—
she knew the peak would be hers
if she painted it often enough,
never sure whether it would be before
or after she passed the threshold.

ii.
We walk behind a hearse drawn
by two perfectly matched black draft horses,
a wagon with window onto followers,
white lilies at the glass
or the petunias she painted in summer,
the scented ones when bunched
at the Santa Fe Opera make heady
the night between acts, sun already down.

iii.
No longer the push to release—
the last painting, sculpture,
blind, those photographed hands
see the peak with Juan at her side
as Stieglitz never would,
bushy hair of the chow brushing
legs bare below a black dress,
black scarf on her head.

One of the Books on the Shelf When Marilyn Monroe Died Was Oppenheimer's *The Open Mind*

You'd expect the plays of Arthur Miller,
which there were, and books on baseball,
but not Oppenheimer's essays from 1946
to 1955, covering the period that ended
in the loss of his security clearance.

By most accounts she was bright,
certainly brighter than she appeared.
Something must have attracted Miller
other than the famous good looks. But
when you look at her now, the breasts

don't seem so large and the face isn't
perfectly symmetrical. Henry Thoreau
has a quote about classical beauty,
questioning the attention and clamor
over what amounts only to extreme

regularity in features, hinting at boredom
underneath. Was it the bright flame that
Oppenheimer had seen? That she saw?
That she knew wasn't going to last? Any
more than the look on Bogart's face as

he stares into her cleavage, Lauren Bacall
at his side. But film captures permanently,
stores for as long as care is taken. And what
after the creator is gone? Those in bright
moments see forward and back in a huge

sweeping glance. It lasts only a second,
but they see their place and it is small and
it is tenuous and it is dependent on their
own nurturing of it—like buildings of adobe.
Eventually they go back to earth.

Fine Scales *Euxoa auxiliaris*

A miller moth perches on my lover's shoulder,
murmurs to him. She lifts dusty, mottled wings,
then closes them to a body not long from cocoon.
It is the heat, the scent he exudes,
closed up in the barrio of the East Side,
curtains drawn because of sensitive eyes,
a place to hide.

Of family *noctuidae*, Moth seeks the night,
fat rich for the migration to mountains
to become grizzly and brown bear feed.
She offers herself to one dangerously thin,
not enough calories despite liquid supplements,
his twist of gut that could as well be strings
of a viola, lower and tougher than a violin.

Yellow and Pink: Elegy for Jackson C.

Yellow breasted finches at the sunflowers,
ones that come to Staab St. in Santa Fe—
yellow of yarrow,
yellow of the beginning of the turn of aspen,
a green lost to too much desert light.

But there is also pink this year—
pink of hollyhocks, cotton candy pink,
Ride the Pink Horse pink,
Zozobra's gloom not yet here,
all those scenes in La Fonda,
old Harvey House hotel,
and in the warren of streets
of this 400 year old town,
the gloom of 50's B&W B-grade films
that is not a gloom as Zozobra,
not an old man consumed by flames,
but the idea of a man who will not die,
who wants to deliver one more line
from the films he spent a life inside.
He's there on the edge of screen
like the cameos of Hitchcock.
I can hear his take, his compare and contrast,
his *You know he played in another film—*
an offering that at the center is pale cream;

then proceeds out until the flickering red
is of a movie run through the projector
over and over until it bursts into flames,
and the theatre goes dark,
and we sit in silence,
filing out when we're absolutely sure
it will not begin again.

Notes

"The Pink Sash": Dialogue on left facing pages is adapted from the short story "The Pink Sash," published in Eleanor Hallowell Abbott's collection, *The Sick-a-Bed Lady*, Grosset & Dunlap Publishers, New York, 1911.

"Recipe for Gold": The recipe is a paraphrase from "Newton's Recipes for Colour and Remedies for Sickness" found in the appendices of *Ghostwalk,* Rebecca Stott, Spiegel & Grau, New York, 2007.

"Stop-Time": Italicized comment is Georgia O'Keeffe's from 1922 accompanying an exhibit of her work together with the photography of Ansel Adams at the Georgia O'Keeffe Museum, Santa Fe, NM, 2008.

"Leaving Raton Pass": Italicized phrase is from "The Prose of the Trans-Siberian and of Little Jeanne of France," Blaise Cendrars, *Blaise Cendrars Complete Poems*, translated from the French by Ron Padgett, University of California Press, Berkeley, California, 1992.

"Before the Levee Comes Down": The levee along the Arkansas River through Pueblo, CO, built for flood control, contained the longest mural in the world. The top layer was taken off for repairs and the height shortened. All the paintings were lost except for a small section that contained ashes of the artist, Judith Pierce.

"Yellow and Pink: Elegy for Jackson C.": Zozobra is an effigy of Old Man Gloom built and burned each year in September in Santa Fe, NM.

Kyle Laws is based out of the Arts Alliance Studios Community in Pueblo, CO where she directs Line / Circle: Women Poets in Performance. Previous collections include *Faces of Fishing Creek* (Middle Creek Publishing), *So Bright to Blind* (Five Oaks Press), and *Wildwood* (Lummox Press). With six nominations for a Pushcart Prize, her poems and essays have appeared in magazines and anthologies in the U.S., U.K., Canada, and France. Granted residencies in poetry from the Massachusetts Museum of Contemporary Art, she is one of eight members of the Boiler House Poets who perform and study at the museum. She is the editor and publisher of Casa de Cinco Hermanas Press.

www.ingramcontent.com/pod-product-compliance
Lightning Source LLC
Chambersburg PA
CBHW020129130526
44591CB00032B/579